D0641127

FROM:

Designed by Heather Zschock

Copyright © 2019
Peter Pauper Press, Inc.
202 Mamaroneck Avenue
White Plains, NY 10601 USA
All rights reserved
ISBN 978-1-4413-2920-2
Printed in China
7 6 5 4 3 2 1

Visit us at www.peterpauper.com

DON'T
WORRY,
BE
present

MINDFULNESS HERE AND NOW

DON'T WORRY,
BE *present*

**MINDFULNESS MEDITATION
DOESN'T CHANGE LIFE.
LIFE REMAINS AS FRAGILE
AND UNPREDICTABLE AS EVER.
MEDITATION CHANGES THE
HEART'S CAPACITY TO
ACCEPT LIFE AS IT IS.**

Sylvia Boorstein

In times of stress and upheaval, it can be difficult to participate in anything beyond restless action. Excessive planning, procrastinating, sleepless nights—these are just some of the ways in which we cope with our daily anxieties. It's true, life can be overwhelming, and so often it can feel like every bad thing happens at once. But you are deserving of peace. You are deserving of all the present joys. And this little book is filled with quotes to remind you of that. Through being aware and mindful of our surroundings, we can see things as they are—honoring our fears as well as the beauty around us that those fears can obscure. For whatever life throws at you, may this volume be a comfort and a reminder to

STAY PRESENT.

THE BEST WAY TO PAY FOR A LOVELY MOMENT IS TO ENJOY IT.

Richard Bach

DO NOT ANTICIPATE TROUBLE, OR WORRY ABOUT WHAT MAY NEVER HAPPEN.

Keep in the sunlight.

BENJAMIN FRANKLIN

FOR FAST-ACTING RELIEF, TRY SLOWING DOWN.

Lily Tomlin

MORE SMILING,
LESS WORRYING.
MORE COMPASSION,
LESS JUDGMENT.
MORE BLESSED,
LESS STRESSED.
MORE LOVE,
LESS HATE.

Roy T. Bennett

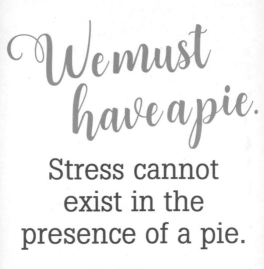

We must have a pie.

Stress cannot exist in the presence of a pie.

David Mamet

TELL YOUR HEART THAT THE FEAR OF SUFFERING IS WORSE THAN THE SUFFERING ITSELF. *Paulo Coelho*

Creative power flourishes only when I am living in the present.

Brenda Ueland

Nothing

CAN BRING YOU PEACE BUT YOURSELF.

Ralph Waldo Emerson

Be not afraid of life.
Believe that life is
worth living,
and your belief
will help create
the fact.

William James

WHAT LIES BEHIND US
AND WHAT LIES BEFORE US
ARE BUT TINY MATTERS
COMPARED TO WHAT
LIES WITHIN US.

Henry S. Haskins

You cannot make yourself feel something you do not feel, but you can make yourself do right in spite of your feelings.

PEARL S. BUCK

MAYBE LIFE DOESN'T
GET ANY BETTER THAN THIS,
OR ANY WORSE, AND WHAT
WE GET IS JUST WHAT
WE'RE WILLING TO FIND:
small wonders,
WHERE THEY GROW.

Barbara Kingsolver

I TELL YOU THE PAST IS A *bucket of ashes.*

CARL SANDBURG

THE IDEAL OF CALM EXISTS IN A SITTING *cat.*

JULES RENARD

YOU CANNOT WAIT FOR AN UNTROUBLED WORLD TO HAVE AN UNTROUBLED MOMENT.

Lemony Snicket

LIKE A

bridge

OVER TROUBLED
WATER,
I WILL EASE YOUR MIND.

Paul Simon

EVERYONE CHASES
AFTER HAPPINESS,
NOT NOTICING THAT
HAPPINESS IS RIGHT
AT THEIR HEELS.

BERTOLT BRECHT

Trust yourself.

YOU KNOW MORE THAN YOU THINK YOU DO.

Dr. Spock

I think it
pisses God off if you
walk by the
color purple
in a field somewhere
and don't notice it.

Alice Walker

EVERYTHING IS CREATED TWICE, FIRST IN THE MIND AND THEN IN REALITY.

ROBIN S. SHARMA

WITHOUT THE DARK, WE'D NEVER SEE *the stars.*

Stephenie Meyer

People are always asking about the good old days. I say, why don't you say *the good now days?*

ROBERT MAXWELL YOUNG

IT IS A MISTAKE
TO LOOK TOO FAR
AHEAD. ONLY ONE
LINK IN THE CHAIN
OF DESTINY CAN
BE HANDLED
at a time.

WINSTON CHURCHILL

HOW WE SPEND OUR DAYS IS, OF COURSE, HOW WE SPEND OUR LIVES. *Annie Dillard*

IN THIS MOMENT, THERE IS PLENTY OF TIME. IN THIS MOMENT, YOU ARE PRECISELY AS YOU SHOULD BE. IN THIS MOMENT, THERE IS

infinite possibility

Victoria Moran

Be grateful
for every hour,
**and accept
what it brings.**

HENRY DAVID THOREAU

When I discover who I am, I'll be free.

RALPH ELLISON

Do not ruin *today* with mourning tomorrow.

Catherynne M. Valente

Much of the secret
of life consists in
knowing how to laugh,
and also how
to breathe.

Alan Watts

WE VASTLY UNDERESTIMATE THE POWER OF TRANSFORMATION OF MIND.

PLACEBOS ARE LIKE THE LOLLIPOP OF OPTIMISM, BUT WE CAN DO MUCH BETTER BY DEALING DIRECTLY WITH THE MIND.

Matthieu Ricard

Don't let a day go
by without asking
who you are...
each time you let
a new ingredient
to enter your
awareness.

Deepak Chopra

IF THE DOORS OF PERCEPTION WERE CLEANSED, EVERYTHING WOULD APPEAR TO MAN AS IT IS: INFINITE.

WILLIAM BLAKE

EACH DAY MEANS A NEW
TWENTY-FOUR HOURS.
EACH DAY MEANS EVERYTHING'S
POSSIBLE AGAIN.
YOU LIVE IN THE MOMENT,
YOU DIE IN THE MOMENT,
YOU TAKE IT ALL

one day at a time.

MARIE LU

Being mindful means that we **suspend judgment for a time**, set aside our immediate goals for the future, and take in the present moment as it is rather than as we would like it to be.

Mark Williams

The most
MAGICAL,
EXQUISITE,
SPONTANEOUS
things happen when
there is no time to
grab your phone.

Taylor Swift

I'M PRETTY MUCH DONE WITH MINDFULNESS. I'M JUST GOING TO START PAYING ATTENTION.

GINA BARRECA

It is the simplest **THINGS IN LIFE THAT HOLD** the most wonder; **THE COLOR OF THE SEA,** the sand between your toes, **THE LAUGHTER OF A CHILD.**

Goldie Hawn

YOU MUST LEARN TO

LET GO.

RELEASE THE STRESS.
YOU WERE NEVER IN
CONTROL ANYWAY.

Steve Maraboli

If you want to *conquer* the anxiety of life, live in the moment, live in the breath.

Amit Ray

IN TIMES OF STRESS,
THE BEST THING WE CAN
DO FOR EACH OTHER IS
TO LISTEN WITH OUR EARS
AND OUR HEARTS
AND TO BE ASSURED THAT
OUR QUESTIONS ARE JUST AS
IMPORTANT AS OUR ANSWERS.

MR. ROGERS

IF YOU REALLY WANT
TO ESCAPE THE THINGS
THAT HARASS YOU,
WHAT YOU'RE NEEDING
IS NOT TO BE IN A
DIFFERENT PLACE BUT
TO BE A DIFFERENT
PERSON.

Seneca

The future
is no place
to place your
better days.

DAVE MATTHEWS

Each morning we
are born again.
*What we do
today*
is what
matters most.

Jack Kornfield

DRINK YOUR TEA
SLOWLY AND
REVERENTLY, AS IF
IT IS THE AXIS ON
WHICH THE WHOLE
EARTH REVOLVES.

Thich Nhat Hanh

Anxiety's like a rocking chair. It gives you something to do, but it doesn't get you very far.

JODI PICOULT

IN THE END THESE THINGS MATTER MOST:

HOW WELL DID YOU LOVE?

HOW FULLY DID YOU LIVE?

HOW DEEPLY DID YOU LET GO? *Jack Kornfield*

Rest is not
idleness, and to
lie sometimes on
the grass under the
trees on a summer's
day, listening to the
murmur of water...
is by no means a
waste of time.

John Lubbock

MAN ONLY LIKES TO COUNT HIS TROUBLES; HE DOESN'T CALCULATE HIS HAPPINESS.

Fyodor Dostoyevsky

LIVE ON, SURVIVE, FOR THE EARTH GIVES FORTH WONDERS. IT MAY SWALLOW YOUR HEART, BUT THE WONDERS KEEP ON COMING. ... WHAT IS EXPECTED OF YOU IS ATTENTION.

Salman Rushdie

Sometimes,
simply by sitting,
the soul collects
wisdom.

ZEN PROVERB

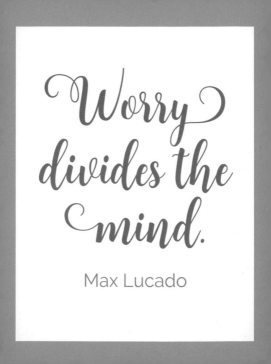

Worry divides the mind.

Max Lucado

EVEN THE DARKEST NIGHT WILL END AND THE SUN WILL RISE. VICTOR HUGO

THE WATER YOU TOUCH
IN A RIVER IS THE
LAST OF THAT WHICH
HAS PASSED, AND THE
FIRST OF THAT WHICH
IS COMING. THUS IT IS
WITH TIME PRESENT.

LEONARDO DA VINCI

Therefore do
not worry about
tomorrow,
for tomorrow will
worry about itself.
Today has enough
trouble of its own.

Matthew 6:34

Return to yourself...
here and now and
when you get there,
you will discover
yourself, like a lotus
flower in full bloom,
even in a muddy pond,
beautiful and strong.

MASARU EMOTO

**TRUE INSTRUCTION
IS THIS:
—TO LEARN TO WISH
THAT EACH THING SHOULD
COME TO PASS AS
IT DOES.**

Epictetus

SO MANY PEOPLE SPEND SO
MUCH OF THEIR LIFE ENERGY
"SWEATING THE
SMALL STUFF"
THAT THEY COMPLETELY
LOSE TOUCH WITH THE
MAGIC AND BEAUTY OF LIFE.

Richard Carlson

Happiness

is a good
flow of life.

Zeno of Citium

The greatest
thing in the
world is to
know how to
belong
to oneself.

Michel de Montaigne

Mindfulness
ISN'T DIFFICULT,
WE JUST NEED TO
remember
TO DO IT.

Sharon Salzberg

THE SUN WILL NOT
RISE OR SET
WITHOUT MY
NOTICE,
AND THANKS.

WINSLOW HOMER

EACH MOMENT IS JUST WHAT IT IS... WE COULD GET DEPRESSED ABOUT IT, OR WE COULD FINALLY APPRECIATE IT AND DELIGHT IN THE PRECIOUSNESS OF EVERY SINGLE MOMENT.

Pema Chödrön

MINDFULNESS

is connected to the heart, to being "heartfelt in the present moment."

Gil Fronsdal

Live today.

NOT YESTERDAY.
NOT TOMORROW.
JUST TODAY.
INHABIT YOUR MOMENTS.
DON'T RENT THEM OUT
TO TOMORROW.

Jerry Spinelli

With every experience, you alone are painting your own canvas, thought by thought, choice by choice.

OPRAH WINFREY

TO A MIND THAT IS STILL, THE WHOLE UNIVERSE SURRENDERS.

Lao Tzu

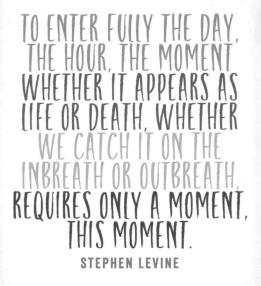

TO ENTER FULLY THE DAY,
THE HOUR, THE MOMENT
WHETHER IT APPEARS AS
LIFE OR DEATH, WHETHER
WE CATCH IT ON THE
INBREATH OR OUTBREATH,
REQUIRES ONLY A MOMENT,
THIS MOMENT.

STEPHEN LEVINE

Do not let yourself be bothered by the inconsequential.

One has only so much time in this world, so devote it... to those you love and things that matter.

Louis L'Amour

A MAN IS LITERALLY
WHAT HE THINKS,
HIS CHARACTER
BEING THE
COMPLETE SUM
OF ALL HIS
THOUGHTS.

James Allen

If it's over,
then don't let
the past screw
up the rest of
your life.

NICHOLAS SPARKS

Do not think of today's failures, but of the **success that may come tomorrow.**

HELEN KELLER

WE CAN COMPLAIN BECAUSE ROSE BUSHES HAVE THORNS, OR REJOICE BECAUSE THORNS HAVE ROSES. *Alphonse Karr*

BE HAPPY FOR THIS MOMENT. THIS MOMENT IS YOUR LIFE.

OMAR KHAYYÁM

WE ARE ALL
IN THE GUTTER,
BUT SOME OF US ARE
looking at
the stars.

Oscar Wilde